SHORT INTRODUCTION
BY
TERRY THE TRASHMAN

This book was written to help you understand the importance of recycling. If we recycle, our world will be a better place in which to live.

Bet you didn't know parts of your bike came from recycled aluminum cans. Did you know that your dark glasses might have been a coke bottle? Did you know that a new yellow dump truck could have come from a plastic water jug?
We also recycle other things like old cars, tires, washers and dryers, wood products and oil.

I will also teach you about those "BAD GUYS" to stay away from. Poison, Pesticides and Cleaning Products, all have labels saying, "WARNING! Keep away from children."

Let's venture down recycle road with me, Terry the Trashman. It'll be fun and rewarding. Are you ready?

Some of the Good Guys you'll meet in this book.

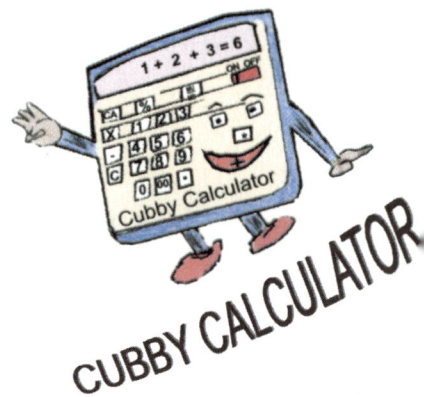

TOONY TV

WORLD FAMOUS

TERRY THE TRASHMAN

RECYCLE

Cubby Calculator

CUBBY CALCULATOR

Pop Can Carl

POP CAN CARL

Please turn lid
Remove lid
Before
Recycling

Pickle Bottle Paulie

PICKLE BOTTLE PAULIE

Mustard Jar Marty

MUSTARD JAR MARTY

It's 5:00 in the morning and
Terry's out on the road.
The Trashman is working to
pick up his load.

15

Hey, Mom !

Put out the garbage can
where it can be seen.
Here comes Terry the Trashman
keeping the neighborhood clean.

Let's learn about some products that come from recyclables. Bats, Rubber Balls, Marbles and Bicycles.

CHECK IT OUT

"NEW" PLASTIC TOYS DOLLS & TRUCKS

GLASS MARBLES

MARBLES

ALUMINUM

BATS & BIKES

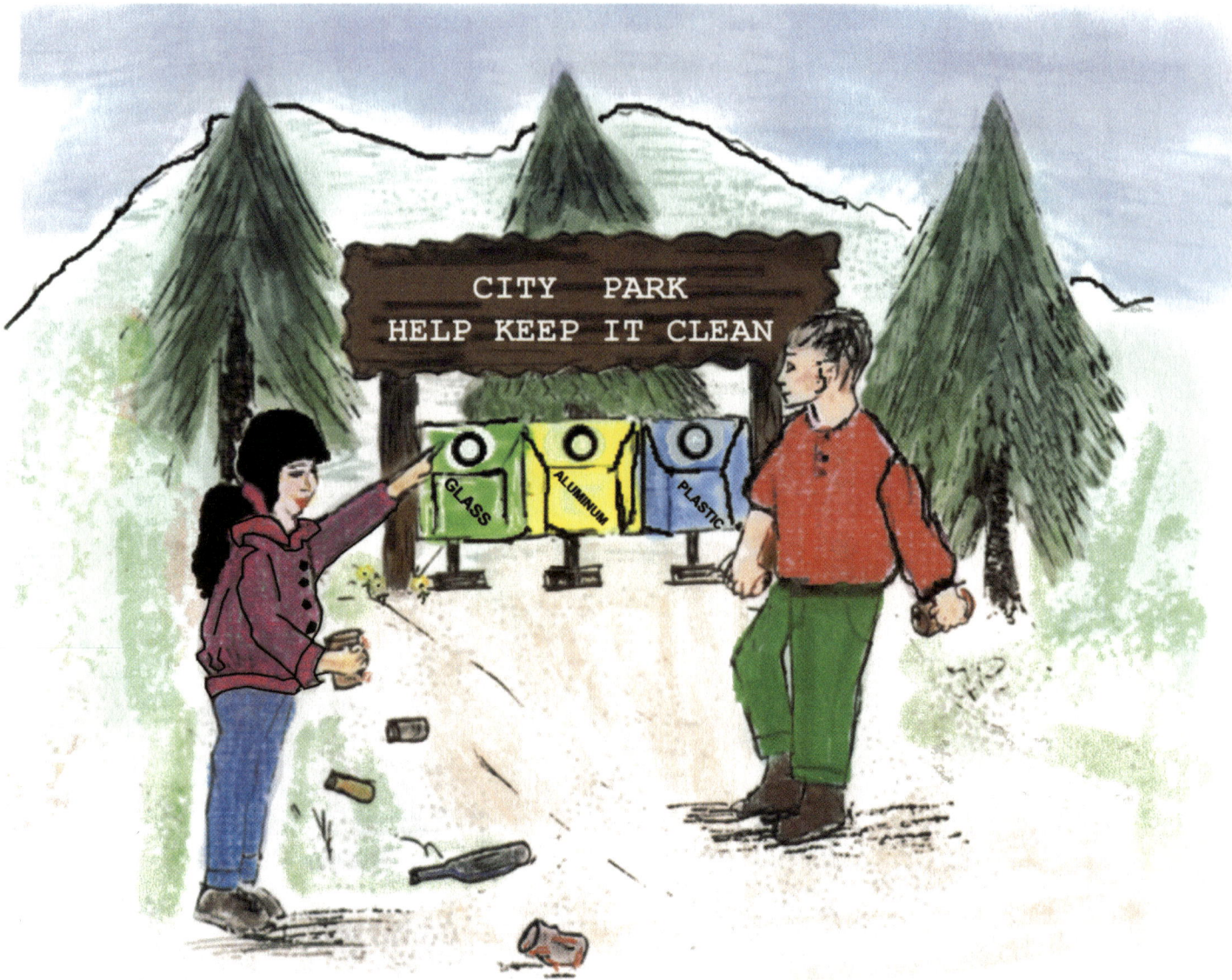

Recycle your cans, recycle your glass,
recycle your plastic bottles too, because
Terry says, "It's the right thing to do."

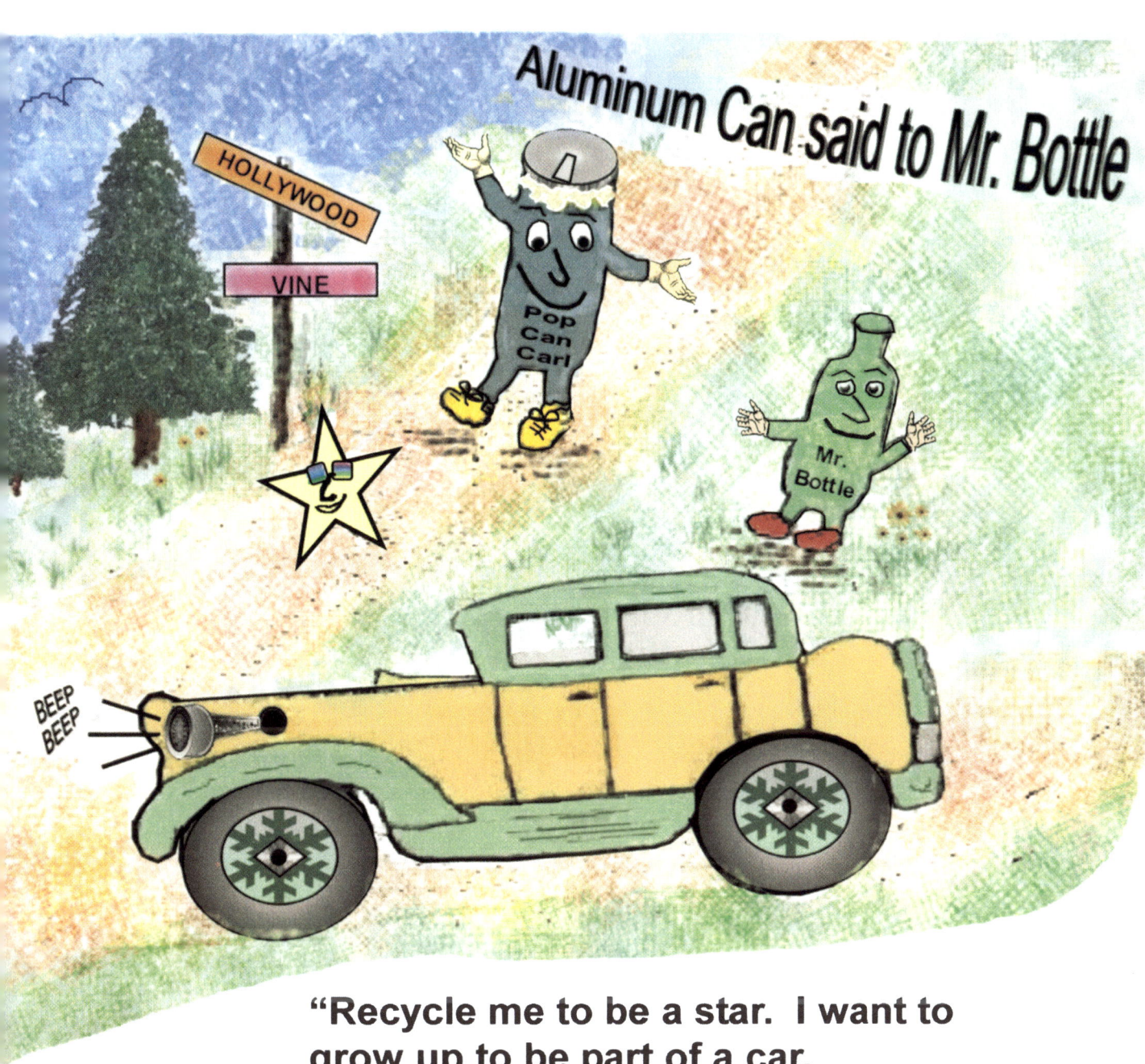

"Recycle me to be a star. I want to
grow up to be part of a car.
Here's a chance for me to transform.
Look at me, I'm an aluminum horn!"

The Glass Bottle said, "Hey, don't forget me. Let me think of what I'd like to be."
"Wow, think of this and don't make fun! I could be your dark glasses to check out the sun."

The plastic jar said, "Give me a turn! Let's think of something to help you learn."

"Practice your numbers; see which is greater. Check me out, I'm a calculator."

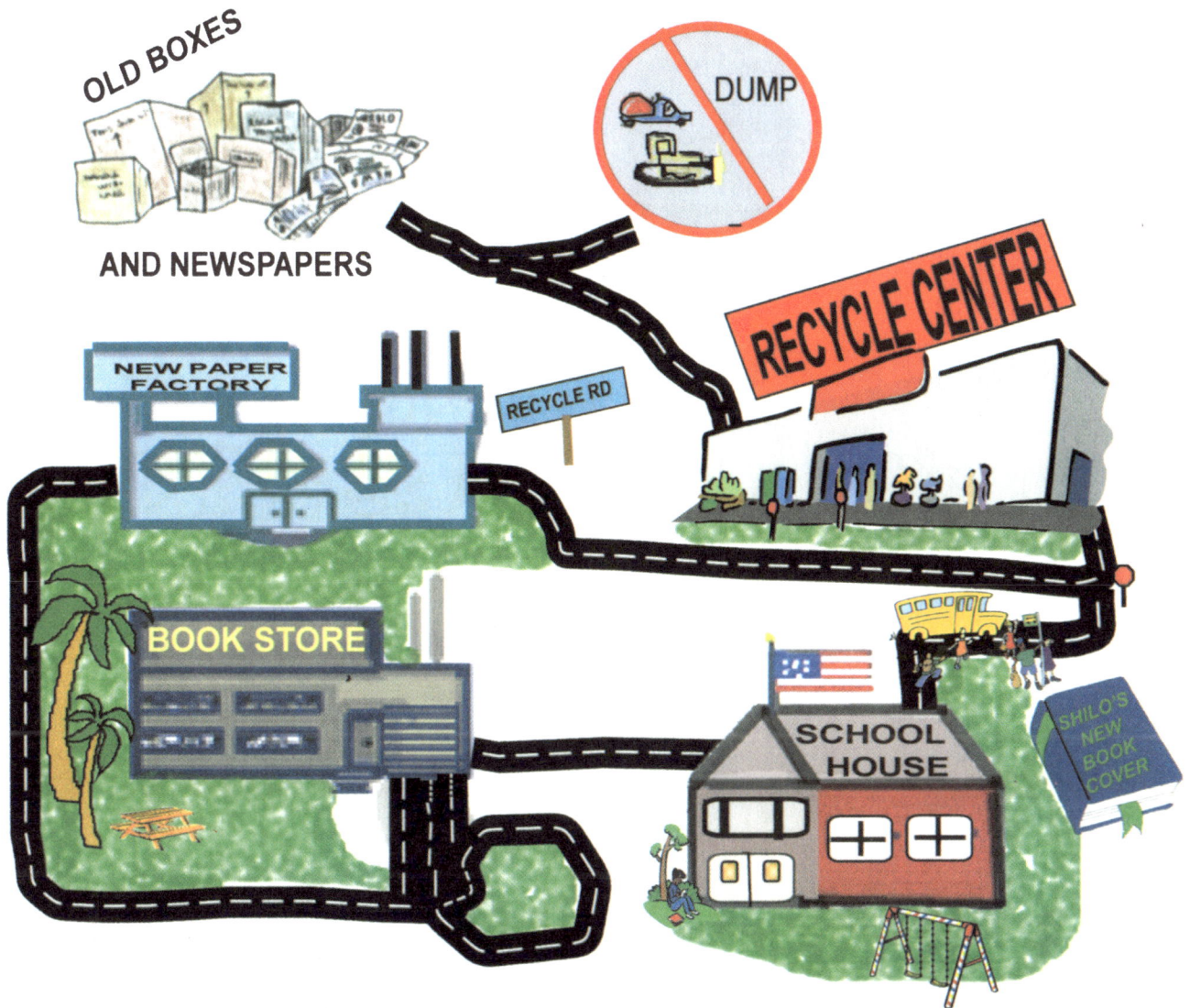

Old boxes and newspapers need a new life, too.
In the dump they'd get cold and come down with the flu.
Save me! Recycle me! Make me brand new!
I want to be your book cover in a pretty shade of blue.

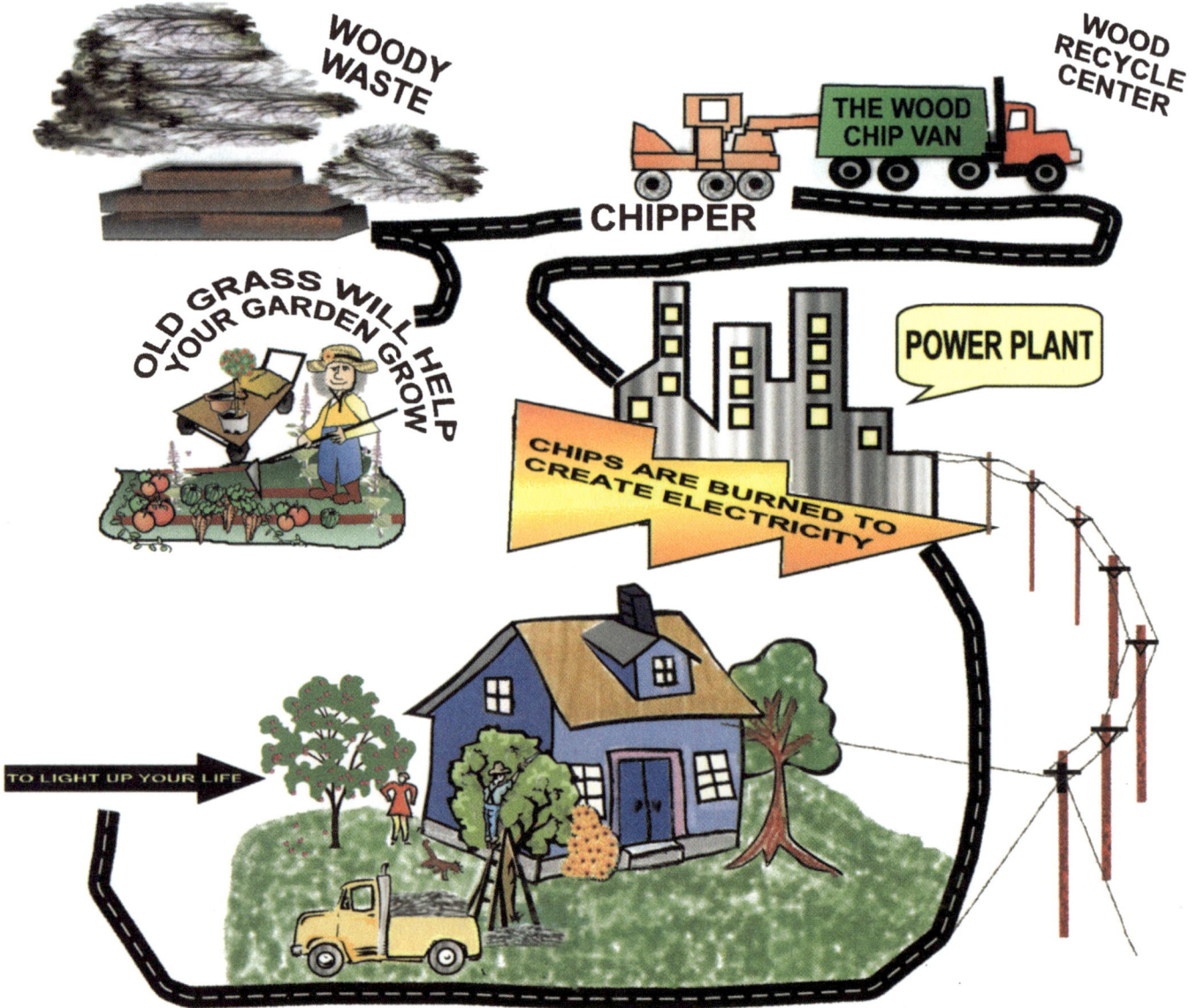

Dad's trimming our trees to help them grow. Let's load his old truck and off we'll go.
Recycle that wood, and don't say we can't! We'll create electricity at our new power plant.

Old cars get crushed, new steel is born.
Let's make a tin can to hold your corn.

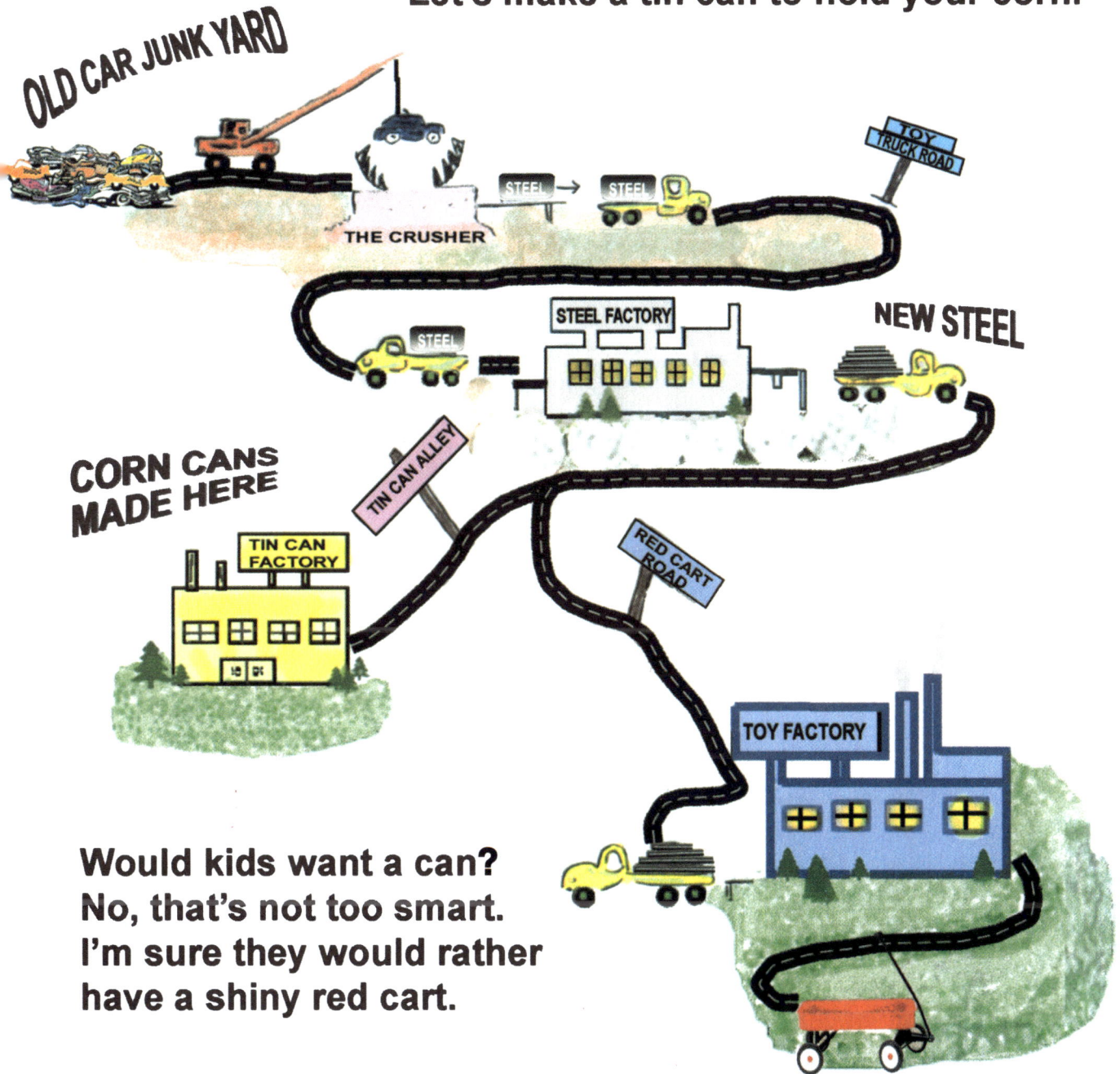

OLD CAR JUNK YARD

TOY TRUCK ROAD

STEEL → STEEL

THE CRUSHER

STEEL FACTORY

NEW STEEL

STEEL

CORN CANS
MADE HERE

TIN CAN ALLEY

TIN CAN
FACTORY

RED CART
ROAD

TOY FACTORY

Would kids want a can?
No, that's not too smart.
I'm sure they would rather
have a shiny red cart.

Skull and cross bones mean "STAY AWAY"; with these ugly guys you do not play! They're old, they're half empty, at home they can't stay. Come Saturday, let's take them to the Hazardous Waste Day.

Tires and oil get recycled too. Refine that oil and make it brand new.

RECYCLE THOSE TIRES!

TIRES CREATE PROTECTIVE GROUND COVER.

SCHOOL PLAYGROUND

DOWN THE DRAIN DON

NO NO NO!

OIL RECYCLE CENTER   TIRE RECYCLE

RECYCLE LANE

Don't put that oil down the drain. We will ship it off to recycle lane.

Electronic products go to E Waste Recycling Centers. "Just ask me," said Toony TV..

TOONY TV

CATHY COMPUTER

VICTOR VCR

VINNEY VIDEO

"Calling all electronics, TV's, microwaves, radios, VCR's, DVD's and all those broken down computers. Let's round them up and take them down to the Electronics Waste Center located in your town."

We'll blow the air horn
and head down the hill.
We're off and running
to the old landfill.

Hey Kids! Remember Terry the Trashman says

"Please recycle because that is good. Thank you for keeping a clean neighborhood."

HEY! IT'S BEEN FUN!

Well, that's it for now. Hope you enjoyed our little adventure down Recycle Road. Keep your eye out for further adventures of Terry the Trashman. See you next time. Please don't forget!

RECYCLE

See ya next week.

ABOUT THE AUTHOR
BY
KATHY LEBLANC
(THE TRASHMAN'S WIFE)

Yes, Virginia, there is a real Terry the Trashman. Terry lives in a small town in the High Sierras of California.

Terry has nicknames such as "Terry the Trashman", "Sierra County Bear Catcher" and "Under-Cover Garbage Cop".

He has done many cancer benefits for children and currently heads up Holiday Planners and Terry's Toys for Tots.

Terry has had signs put up at his transfer stations and the local landfill that read "We recycle Toys for Tots". He has saved the lives of many toys headed for disaster, and has made many kids happy.

Terry performs recycling programs in our schools in Sierra County. He loves kids and people in general. He put his ideas in text so that people of all ages can enjoy them.

Learning To Recycle with Terry The Trashman

Terry LeBlanc
P.O. Box 387
Loyalton, CA 96118
Phone 530-993-0247
Fax 530-993-4648

Printed in the USA by
Auburn Printers & Integrated Marketing
www.auburnprinters.com

NICE MEETING YA!

SEE YA NEXT TIME.

The End.

P.S.
If you're wondering, yes, this
book is printed on recycled paper.

ISBN 0-9755913-0-4
9 780975 591307

90000